CN00894012

This delightful book is the latest in the series of Ladybird books which have been specially planned to help grown-ups with the world about them.

As in the other books in this series, the large clear script, the careful choice of words, the frequent repetition and the thoughtful matching of text with pictures all enable grown-ups to think they have taught themselves to cope. The subject of the book will greatly appeal to grown-ups.

Series 999

THE LADYBIRD
BOOKS FOR GROWN–UPS SERIES

THE ZOMBIE
APOCALYPSE

by

J.A. HAZELEY, N.S.F.W. and J.P. MORRIS, O.M.G.
(Authors of 'Mole Machine Projects For Small Gardens')

Publishers: Ladybird Books Ltd., Loughborough
Printed in England. If wet, Italy.

When there is no more room in Hell, the dead will walk the earth.

But there are still lots of interesting things you can do.

During a zombie apocalypse, shops may reduce their opening hours, telephone and broadband coverage is likely to be patchy and the police may be very busy.

Minor crimes such as looting can be easily dealt with by neighbours working together.

It could be secret military experiments or a viral pandemic. It might be cosmic rays or reading some Latin—style words aloud from a forbidden codex.

It could even be a fungal infection like athlete's foot, but one that explodes mushrooms through your face and makes you eat everybody.

There are so many ways for people to turn into zombies.

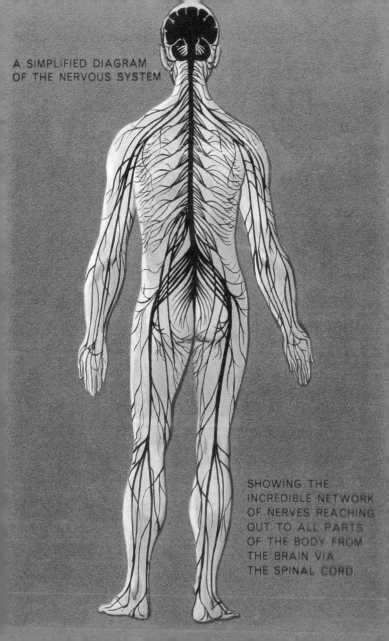

A SIMPLIFIED DIAGRAM
OF THE NERVOUS SYSTEM

SHOWING THE
INCREDIBLE NETWORK
OF NERVES REACHING
OUT TO ALL PARTS
OF THE BODY FROM
THE BRAIN VIA
THE SPINAL CORD

In an emergency, the authorities use secret phrases to alert one another without panicking the public.

Stay informed by listening for coded announcements such as "Inspector Sands has risen from the grave" and "Would Doctor Strong please return to the morgue?"

The walking dead spend a lot of time bashing themselves against windows.

Maybe it is all the flies in their brains.

Len has gathered a group of fellow survivors together. He would defend them with his life.

"We are like a family," says Len, proudly.

Len never talked to his real family much before the world ended, which made it easier to bludgeon his slavering mother to a pulp yesterday with a tent mallet.

"That man is waving, Dad," says Leo. "He might need help."

"Take the controls, Leo," says Dad. "We cannot be too careful."

Katie is excited. Dad has never taken a headshot from this distance before.

Zombies like shopping centres. There are so many inside this one that the best idea is to blend in.

Shamble around. Slump on a bench. Go glassy-eyed. Moan and drool. Smear your face with ketchup.

Just like you might normally do in a shopping centre.

Lara has constructed her own home-made flame-thrower.

The flame-thrower has turned the walking corpses into burning walking corpses. Now everything they touch catches fire.

"This did not happen with the cricket bat," thinks Lara.

Todd has spent his whole life worrying about what he would do in the event of zombie attack.

Terrorism, nuclear proliferation, environmental collapse and global inequality seem so unimportant now.

Todd is glad he did not waste any of his life worrying about them.

What will it be like after the end of the world?

Maybe colourful gangs of crazy looters will chase each other in souped—up ultra-trucks covered in spikes and guns.

Or maybe they won't.

Giles and Peter are civil servants.

They hid in the basement of the Treasury when the rest of the government started eating each other. Now they are all that is left.

Giles and Peter have found two white coats and a pile of cones.

"Order will be restored soon," says Giles, hopefully.

"Is the sun meant to be like that, Dad?" asks Alfie.

Alfie and Dad run.

Conlan and Degsy are raiding a stockade. They have killed everyone using their spades and can now look for food.

They have found one box of tins and one box of salted peanuts.

This box contains dozens of human ears. They will not take this box.

Dickon has found a telephone box and is calling for help.

The emergency services are out of action and he cannot remember anybody's number because he usually uses a smart-phone.

"Maybe one of the ladies on these post-cards can help," thinks Dickon.

Some people say civilisation after a zombie apocalypse will go back to The Stone Age.

Nobody tidies up or collects the bins. The electricity keeps going off. There are dead bodies piled up in the streets.

It is actually more like the 1970s.

In films about zombies, people do foolish things.

They go down into the fruit cellar for safety. They hope a bite will get better in the morning. They think growling, drooling men are probably just tramps.

People in zombie films have not watched enough zombie films.

Sebastian is manning the Ventnor comms station on the Isle of Wight.

An island is a safe place to be because it is easily quarantined, but supplies from the mainland can be irregular.

If the islanders find out Sebastian is hoarding the last roll of toilet paper, they will break in and kill him.

Toby is a vegetarian and will not eat rat. He has been looking for fresh vegetables for weeks.

Yesterday he found a botany laboratory. It was full of walking, stinging plants.

Toby now has a heightened sense of hearing, and irony.

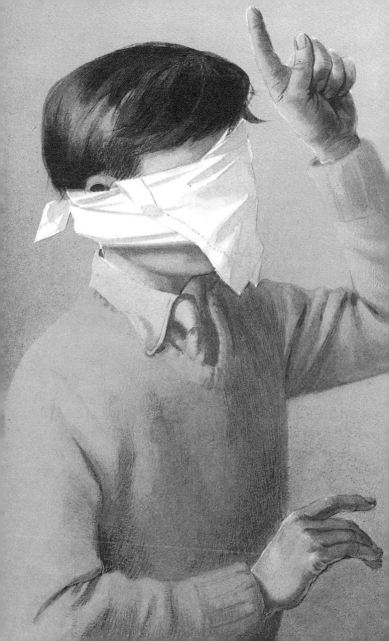

Andy finds it easier to shoot zombies in the head if he pretends he is playing a video game.

The baddies in video games were often zombies.

This is because zombies bought far fewer video games than Russians, Germans, terrorists or robots.

William and his family have found a beautiful patch of countryside, free from infection.

"No explosions or screams," says William, "just bird–song."

A colony of infected bats can reduce a human body to a skeleton in twenty minutes.

"Careful!" says Catherine. "This house is booby–trapped."

The children step over the trip wire at the front door.

If they are lucky, they will find food and ammunition inside.

If they are very lucky, the cat that just jumped through the window will not set off the rest of the traps.

The sun is going down.

"I do hope we see it come up again tomorrow," says Mark.

"So do I," says Joanne.

Mark and Joanne double—check the nails around the window.

Yesterday, all the water caught fire.

Today, the Very Big Bees are coming.

The end of the world is full of surprises.

THE AUTHORS would like to record their gratitude and offer their apologies to the many Ladybird artists whose luminous work formed the glorious wallpaper of countless childhoods. Revisiting it for this book as grown-ups has been a privilege.

MICHAEL JOSEPH

UK | USA | Canada | Ireland | Australia
India | New Zealand | South Africa

Michael Joseph is part of the Penguin Random House group of companies whose addresses can be found at global.penguinrandomhouse.com

Penguin
Random House
UK

First published 2016
001

Copyright © Jason Hazeley and Joel Morris, 2016
All images copyright © Ladybird Books Ltd, 2016

The moral right of the authors has been asserted

Printed in Italy by L.E.G.O. S.p.A

A CIP catalogue record for this book is available from the British Library

ISBN: 978–0–718–18445–2

www.greenpenguin.co.uk

MIX
Paper from
responsible sources
FSC® C018179

Penguin Random House is committed to a sustainable future for our business, our readers and our planet. This book is made from Forest Stewardship Council® certified paper.